Gothic Poetry

by

Strange Nocturnal

The Gathering Of Gargoyles

The storm raged on and had done for nights,

as prophesized by long gone minds,

for what they built was far from left behind,

through the ages had stood the tests of time.

The structure firm and solid still,

designed by a long forgotten will,

artistry and a conjuring yet to reveal,

for now the storm was strong,

passing upon the occult building in the wilderness away
from modern mortals,

when suddenly the first bolt through the sky shone,

striking the highest part of the building,

no longer in the darkness,

no longer just a figure hidden,

for in that flash of light,

that came crashing through the night,

to meet with one stone carved winged being.

As the rain poured down its eyes

and as the wind it now did cry,

for now this creature was alive.

Its wings embraced it, for now it could feel,

breathed in the immortal breath, to feel the beating pulse,

did spread its wings and lifted its clawed feet and arisen
from the roof.

Suspended in the air, its eyes seeked here and there,

meeting its stoney stare, more eyes of stone beneathe,

they where like itself but not moving like it was.

Lightening strook it again, down onto the roof it fell, back to where it came,

this time, it felt the pain,

remembering again its birth, the birth not from this night,
but of many and more memories flooded unto it,

as it sit it rose once again.

The second strike of life this night did awaken the eyes,
the others now blinked and cried and more winged beings
took to the skies,

It joined them up, then raced further past the storm and
the others followed the first born,

For they would be loyal,

as their creator and creation was intended.

They rise from the structure now each night,

to settle down by daylight.

The gathering of Gargoyles.

The Vampyres Taste

The vampire tired of thirst for blood,

the vampires thirst grew for love.

Immortality alone, for its vitality,

passing through centuries, likened to a mortals days,

for the ways of mortals, although not one, could relate,

long now gone since death as mortals would call it, be put to date.

No stranger to myths of its kind, displeased by the ignorance of their sublime,

wished to be loved not rejected as some monster wrapped in writings and pictures moving for some money to be made, yet they called them monsters, for it seen what they prey upon.

A chance the vampire had to right this wrong, then perhaps in a future gone,

love could be had for the vampire, as the vampires song, would be sung.

The night with beauty changed its ways,

for in eternal darkness, would they vow to never be
heartless,

ever beating blood and flow,

flew in time to be entwined with immortal night.

Mortals of the Vampyre did write:

That vampires fear or scarcely touched by sunlight...

This Vampyre does know!

The Stars! The Moon!

Reflections in the waters bloom!

Then what of crucifixs..

Yet more myths with mixtures!

In the eyes of the Vampyre many things did cross or was
crossed, mortals with their story telling lost!

The thirst as for a mortal, water and liquids to replenish as
to sustain their mortality, Yes to the Vampyre blood is a
necessity!

Sleeping in coffins, as a bed is a coffin if mortals cease to be so in a wooden frame, yet to a myth bring more to a mortal than fame.

No sunlight does not turn the Vampyre to flame!

A stake through the heart or beheading, what doeth immortal mean or is it mortal forgetting!

So think once more and think again,

for as the fangs strikes the vein.

The Vampyre lives

and lives again!

With Love in heart, yes we too have a soul and to be together to walk the dark,

turning the one that knows this well, for the re-telling of a un-dying love that lasts beyond the grave, surely the Vampyre would save.

Howl to the Moon

Darting and dashing through mud and past fallen leaves,
scratched by branches of bare trees,

blooded and breathing heavy, must keep running, must
escape this beast,

it follows behind the scent I leave.

The clouds part for a moment steady,

the full moon shines upon this now open territory.

I must be ready, the beast on all fours fastens pace,

for this life has now become a race,

between man and beast,

the man wished not to become a living feast,

running through the open,

the moon high,

dare to look back one more time,

nigh keep going on till the moon is no more and the beast
gone!

Run so I did and run, but the moons glow bright,

not having to look back into the night, could feel its eyes
upon thy prey, for now I pray these legs can keep,

but now its breath I feel,

then bite sudden and deep,

laying looking up,

for what changes soon,

They Howl to the Moon!

Where Witches Merry Meet

Cloaked and leaving their abode,

not one for taking treacherous roads,

upon a broom she rode,

to and through the air!

Her stocking'd feet brushed past tops of trees,

cauldron on the back making a beat, she sang an
enchantment,

to which her cat purred back,

t'was the sabbath night,

such a magickal delight,

to congregate in flight,

nearing their destination, all sang together,

then to stand upon the earth once more,

around the poof of smoke and boom a fire did light,

the cauldron warming with potion brewing,

the stars did shine bright above,

for only they knew what was to be instore,

divination, mischief making, a love spell, a heart breaking, a hex if vexed, or curse if worse, who knoweth apart from the witches,

who knows what pleasures or pain but they,

who knoweth where they landeth on their feet,

or what contents brewed in their cauldrons deep,

only witches know!

Where witches go!

What magick they sow!

Where witches merry meet

and merry meet again!

Have You Lost If You Ever Loved At All?

Have you lost if you ever loved at all?

Beauty Brought Me Here

Beauty brought me here,

through the maze of fear,

I braved the nightmare,

just to get near!

Beauty brought me here!

Beauty brought me here!

Through never ending dark you did shon (shine),

so bright your light I did gaze upon,

Are you really real?!

What's this feeling that I feel!

When we touch,

a longing embrace,

only closing our eyes to dim our shine,

while our lips lock in each others taste,

for this kiss captures time,

our time,

one to remember for all of time,

for your beauty is so much more,

now I give you this heart it's yours,

its's out from the dark!

I give it through art!

Would you be as so kind to reply, not just so one could call you mine!

Your beauty brought me here.

One True Kiss and the Curse Will Lift!

Follow your heart,

through the dark,

let it guide your way,

but never lead you astray,

brave the burning light of cursed days,

be balanced with your dark side,

even on blessed nights,

keep what is wild and untamed,

for this love is eternally unleashed,

furiously passionate,

calm and quite in late,

together always,

the souls will never part ways,

though for times nightmares must be endured and for
moments others will mock, judge and damn!

For loving I am damned,

for fear of losing you,

they say we lost each other,

is it a curse to think of our forever.

Only true love can break this curse,

they make us question,

what if true love is worse,

they try to take our love and make it tainted and perverse,

the kiss sends me into a blaze,

yet I shiver whenever I am near her,

torture is what I knew before this in daze,

she wakes me when I sleep,

her tease is like the only cure for this disease,

I'll only give up on my knees,

for she is my only defeat,

I'll love her, even when I'm deceased,

just one true kiss and the curse will lift,

undo what evil hath been done,

only true love can break this curse,

without love,

there is nothing worse,

why curse it,

why damn it,

when we need more love in the world.

Just one kiss, her kiss and any evil spell will lift,

for only true love is the truest gift.

One true kiss and the Curse Will Lift.

A Funeral Forecast

Magickal, majestic and mystical, monstrous mountains
and streams, forests, lakes and rivers near,

old towns, valleys, villages and onwards to the sea.

Weathered days and forgotten times passed,

when death did upon the mortal soul had called,

in a wooden box below earth the coffin had fallen,

nothing now but a stone a name, no one left now to bare
their memory.

The corpses rotten remains for nights and deaths days,

deranged in povertys peace,

down in earth deep.

In the churchyard the graves resided, a resident on the far
corner of the cemetery cold,

where splendors of autumns orange leaves that few
mourners only see,

in the water weaving from the wind and weather beaten
trees,

natures show of life and death most beautifully flowed,

on the far corner of the cemetery cold,

falling and coursing the rivers rising,

the heavens exploded and with hells wrath,

heavy rains enraged and was now exposing,

eroding the hallowed soil on the far corner of the cemetery cold.

Allowing this forgotten soul to travel water not seen nor touched,

since life long ago.

Where this wooden box, boat and home,

of my death and remains unknown.

For my will left my body, long ago.

Night Terror!

Night terror, blackness from behind.

The back of the mind.

Blackness, shadows, myths and monsters!

Night terrors, beheaded blind, memories haunting!

Night Terror!

Night Terror!

Falling forever!

Wake wet, frozen!

Night terror, mixed memories,

unconsciousness, uncontrolled!

Dark cold and alone!

Shiver into cruelness, consciousness now.

Night terror.... Night terror!

The Dueling Wizard And Warlock

The duel of eons and dimensions,

A Wizard! A Warlock!

Locked in battle, weapons of staffs, words,

rituals, wands, alchemy, looks and gestures.

Conjuring energy, spirits the spectrum.

Gods, demons, deities, of all and ancient nations.

Their strategy sorcery, power of creation,

destruction beyond imagination.

They battle with knowledge of forces unseen.

A Wizard, A Warlock,

breaking all laws.

A Wizard!

A Warlock!

An Infinite war!

Horror Nation

Poltergeist politicians,

ghost governments,

bloody handed bankers,

ectoplasmic economy,

skeleton society,

horror nation.

A island on which the monsters reside in.

Horror nation.

A Forest Fairy

Of all the forests I did roam,

only one, a fairy, in my sights did glow.

A forest fairy, mischievous in flight!

I remember a forest fairy fluttering in the light,

I remember a forest fairy dancing at night!

Forrest fairy, how many years it's been.

Sometimes visits me in my dreams.

Enchanted Sleep takes hold

From windows darkness dances,

flames flicker shadows onto chamber walls,

enchanted, before sleep takes hold,

rain falls on glass payne it pours,

solitude in ambience,

comfortable and so vulnerable.

Enhchanted sleep takes hold.

In The Cemetery Rows

Ivory bones, beneathe the grey,

moss bound tombstones,

six feet or more and death bestowed,

a widowed wife pays her grief with a red rose,

alone she lets her tears flow,

she still wears her funeral robes to visit her long lost love,

even though it was many moons ago,

tormented by the thought of her lovers remains out there
she must go,

her soulmate wanders the afterlife without her physically,

yet in the isolation, her salvation, she knows,

death did not part their love in spirit,

with death love changes and still grows,

and finds comfort in the peace of the necropolis,

as she will reside by her lovers side, together in time,

together in the cemetery rows.

The Haunted Hall

It was as if winter came all in one moment,

in the ruined old grounds, of a once noble home,

doubting my senses I reached into darkness to touch bare
walls of stone,

I came out to see for myself, investigate on my own,

I scaled the walls, that once hid a queen of old, history
had its dungeons filled within,

lords and ladies ruled with their lives, deaths and
tragedies,

all in this place I was told had unfold,

I stumbled into once busy corridors and passage ways,

banquet rooms and chambers I walked,

but was in the shallow dark dungeons, a voice from the
emptiness did talk,

feminine and enchanting, unexpected and unexplainable,

I tried to speak but the air, frozen cold,

the words lost in trembling thought,

and in my vision an apparition,

paralyzed with fear, the spectre came forward,

in the phantom I was caught,

no tuition of this had I recollection, so no response to me was taught,

moaning suddenly as it jumped near,

my then sweaty hands and fingers climbed the rattling shackles in the walls,

grabbing them I picked myself up of the floor and ran out the dungeon door,

dizzily with blood burning through icy veins,

my beating body with will alone,

I escaped the ruined old grounds of a once noble home,

and now I know,

that it was true what I had been told,

about the haunted hall of old.

Murder At The Crossroads

Unmarked graves pave the way to the crossroads,

weathered noose ropes swing from the half burnt trees,

by the very same crossroads,

no one ever stops here,

no one who sets foot where the roads meet,

ever leaves,

if you pass through at night you will hear their mighty
cry,

the cry of a thousand victims,

their souls tortured and tormented,

carried by the cursed flock of crows,

the crows that call for more,

the very same crows that called you hear to lose,

to the murder at the crossroads.

The Crimson Prison

No escape was certain, there was no way out,

screams and torments over years,

these walls have heard,

their will breaking with pleas of insanity screaming,

the nightmares echo and shout constantly self sentencing,

the damned bars and walls of the crimson prison,

red with diversity like the detainees previous,

the damned within only know the suffering felt inside us,

there's something serious underlying and insidious,

rusty bars and chains aren't the only iron evidence
shackled,

splashed and splattered about this red cell,

this red cell is my own isolation, no rest or forgiveness in
my own solitary secluded hell,

the crimson prison, the crimes, the piercing vision and
sick minds that committed them,

sometime suicide burns at the back of the mind like a victim,

no peace to find and no hope knowing the next place you are going is no better,.

Just punishment forever with the bloody crimes in this damned crimson prison

Letting Go

Letting go is never really letting go,

over time seems long ago,

but looking back it's more like harboring so many,

what could have beens?

& lost dreams.

The Ground We Stand Upon

Open eyes see the lands in which lives have lived, loved
and died,

closed eyes remain life giving and cried,

the mind open and heart feeling,

realizes the histories upon which makes the current state
of events equate,

the relation of the ground we stand upon,

the countless dead beneath buried in the earth and rotten
high on which we create our times,

let us not forget the events and loss to which without,

our futures could not ride,

when next looking at the soil remember,

it's that connecting us to our mortal coil,

that we go back to like the crashing of a tide.

Society Screams Too Many Monsters

Of everything imaginable is almost entirely possible,

the thoughts of the impossible probable,

society screams,

Too many Monsters!

A-List serial killers and criminals revealed in writings,

forever frightenly entertaining with warning and caution,

Too many Monsters,

society screams,

the cause gets diluted,

the people deluded,

the victims and the monsters like one executed,

who's in charge here?

Society screams,

Too many Monsters!

A Lonely Spirit Does Roam

Escaping the shell,

wandering alone,

like ash to ground, fire to fuel, smoke to air,

finally a place with no fare,

heaven and hell are nowhere now,

no wondering who, what, where or how?

Limitlessness, endlessly wrapped in solitude

that which is and is not,

not new but a home,

no walls or doors,

just the great beyond,

the countless unknown.

A lonely spirit does roam.

A Sinister Seance

Mourners gather mourning,

on the anniversary of the one they once loved and knew,

years passed since they departed few,

gathered on a autumn night,

they come to communicate with all their might,

around a table,

in a circle,

they hold hands and the medium travels,

calling out their lover still living and in a death like state,

without the manifestation of their love,

cries and cries to the heavens above,

the medium moans and moves,

an eerie mist swarms the room,

hands locked in astonishment and amazed,

they all watch and gaze awaiting an apparition,

the table, then doors and windows move,

the lover starts to swoon,

medium drops suddenly, head hitting cold table top,

all activity dramatically stops,

the lover recovers and demands,

"Keep tight hold! Don't break the circle, keep the energy
and keep holding hands!"

The mist like substance begins to wrap weave and dance,

"Is that you my everything?!"

The lover asked,

the medium shuddered and raised their head,

the medium but not in their own voice then said,

"I am not known by the living and I've never been dead"

The mist grew like shadow and that shadow was darker
than the dark within the room and that darkness grew and
grew,

don't break the circle the medium understands,

"We've crossed a boundary and it must be binded back to
whence it came"

the shadow like demon made a noise that of unlike

anything heard by worldly ears,

then in our tongue did state,

"How can you banish that which hath no name?"

the medium replied

"We have names for what you are!"

the anonymous entity seemed to smile,

then said,

"You dabble in things you do not know,

you question where will you go?

So I am here to show you!"

www.ingramcontent.com/pod-product-compliance
Lightning Source LLC
La Vergne TN
LVHW051712080426
835511LV00017B/2881